ONE SIMPLE PHRASE

Also by Sue Giannini

Overcoming Mediocrity Remarkable Women

Also by Christie Ruffino

Dare to Be a Difference Maker – Volume II
Treasured Tribes
Overcoming Mediocrity Series

ONE SIMPLE PHRASE

One Woman's Journey to Overcome Mediocrity and Never Give Up!

Susan Giannini & Christie Ruffino

DPWN Publishing

Copyright © 2022 by Christie Ruffino

DPWN Publishing supports copyright. Copyright fuels creativity, encourages diversity, promotes free speech, and creates a vibrant culture. Thank you for buying an authorized edition of this book and for complying with copyright laws by not reproducing, scanning, storing, copying, or distributing any part of this book in any form for public or private use without the written permission of the copyright owner.

This is a work of nonfiction. The authors in this book have shared their stories according to their memories. While all the stories are true, the names and identifying details may have been changed to protect the privacy of the people involved. Any resulting resemblance to persons living or dead, is entirely coincidental and unintentional.

Front cover and book design by DPWN Publishing

Published by DPWN Publishing
A division of the Dynamic Professional Women's Network, Inc.
1879 N. Neltnor Blvd. #316, West Chicago, IL 60185
www.OvercomingMediocrity.org
www.OurDPWN.com

Printed in the United States of America

ISBN: 978-1-939794-27-7

A Psalm of David

The LORD is my shepherd, I lack nothing.

He makes me lie down in green pastures,
he leads me beside quiet waters,

he refreshes my soul.
He guides me along the right paths for his name's sake.

Even though I walk through the darkest valley, I will fear no evil, for you are with me; your rod and your staff, they comfort me.

You prepare a table before me in the presence of my enemies.
You anoint my head with oil, my cup overflows.

Surely your goodness and love will follow me all the days of my life, and I will dwell in the house of the LORD forever.

—Psalm 23 (NIV)

Table of Contents

Foreword by Christie Ruffino 1

Stories Before the Story 9

    Lawrence Giannini 11

    Gerard Ruffino 13

    Jesica Ruffino 15

    Jan Blackburn Sawitoski 17

    Deana Dolan 19

    More Tributes 21

Quote 23

One Simple Phrase by Sue Giannini 25

About Sue Giannini 35

Your Stories About Sue 41

Foreword

by Christie Ruffino (Daughter)

I have to keep wiping away the tears to write this foreword, just hours after the passing of my best friend, my confidant, my advisor, my encourager, and my number one fan, my mom, Susan Jean Giannini (Crowley).

We all come head-to-head with challenging seasons like this at one point or another. Sometimes, the loss can come like an unexpected tsunami in the night, or it can come gently, at daybreak, like a sweet summer rain.

I am happy to say my mom's final passing was sweet because the last few moments of her life here on earth were, but the months and years leading up to that point, were not so nice. She suffered from an endless array of physical and emotional challenges that left her and our whole family feeling frustrated, helpless, and sad.

My mom was a beautiful and strong woman, who to this day, I still admire very much. I hope you read her story, *One Simple Phrase,* on the following pages of this book about her journey of strength and resilience. It

One Simple Phrase

was written back in 2016 when her story was featured on the pages of our Overcoming Mediocrity Remarkable Women book. Since then, she was riddled with a never-ending list of physical afflictions ranging from a major back surgery, dementia, Sjogren's Syndrome, Lupus, RA, countless UTIs, and numerous blood transfusions that led to the final ailments that plagued her body, kidney failure and an infectious blood disease. All while still battling depression which only escalated during her final days in complete isolation due to the pandemic.

The family would try to encourage her to stay strong, and she would gear up for the next battle, only to be knocked down again by something new and overwhelming. I can't imagine what she went through and how I would have responded if I had been quarantined, in her condition, away from my family for 11 straight weeks in the hospital. I know how hard it was for us not to be able to see her, be with her, hold her hand, bring her flowers, comfort her, and remind her that she wasn't alone. But how did "she" feel? How could "she" remain strong without the physical ability to even get out of bed, staring at the ceiling for what must have seemed to her an eternity?

She wanted to give up. At times, pleading with her family for it to be over. But even though she simply had to request for her nutrition to be stopped, she refrained from doing so to protect us from having to navigate through yet another emotional layer of the equation. A layer that she had to face years before with the loss of her father and brother, which you can read about in her story.

Sue Giannini & Christie Ruffino

I am both happy and heartbroken to say that on Friday, May 8th, 2020, my mom, Susan Giannini's mission here on earth was over. The day prior, her family was called to decide whether to start kidney dialysis or not. The hospital had agreed to let us see her, completely gowned up and masked, before making such a difficult yet life-changing decision. What would we do? Her kidneys were failing, and she could not continue without dialysis. Would that be what she wanted? Was that the right decision or not? We were excited to see and be with her after such a long time, but we were anxious about the decision we faced.

Very early the next morning, we got a call to come sooner. Mom's condition was failing fast, and we needed to make that decision sooner than initially thought. We had no idea what to expect when we arrived at the hospital.

Death is a process. When we were finally able to see mom, we were informed that her body had already started that process. We no longer had to decide about dialysis. We had to accept the fact that she now needed hospice care. We simply had to be with her, love her, comfort her, and cherish her during her final days.

Fortunately for us, (and her) mom transitioned into heaven less than three hours after we arrived at her side.

We were in the process of preparing to have her transported to a hospice facility because the doctors told us the process could take days or even weeks. We wanted her to have the best care during that time, but I believe she could hear us talking and wanted to spare us from grieving any longer.

One Simple Phrase

I find comfort in believing she was ready to go home, and hearing our voices gave her the comfort she needed to take that final step.

I was holding her hand, her husband was stroking her head, and we were talking about fond memories as she silently took her final breath.

Susan Jean Giannini (Crowley) was survived by her husband, Lawrence Giannini, two children, Christie Ruffino (Vodden) and Gerald Vodden, and stepson Larry Giannini. She was a devoted grandmother to Gerald Ruffino, Jesica Ruffino, and Matthew Vodden and a step-grandmother to Joshua Giannini, Christopher Giannini, Anthony Giannini, Sidney Giannini. And finally, she had two great-grandchildren, Scarlet Clark, and Joey Clark, and one crazy-ass rescue cat named Sammy.

Sue loved her family, her friends, and her pets. She enjoyed gardening and going to Friday night dinner and movies with her girlfriends. And in her better years, she especially loved babysitting her grandkids, going to Las Vegas, and spending the weekends at the rickety old cabin they had in Delhi, Iowa.

The fondest memories of my mom are of her carefree, crazy, and loving side. She was always the fun mom who played Jethro Tull and the Beatles when I was a teenager, always laughing and enjoying life. When I went through a terrible divorce, she was my rock. She cried with me, grieved with me, and encouraged me to endure every horrible thing I faced during that battle. She was my always-available babysitter and role model as I raised my kids alone. She taught me how to be a good mom and a terrific grandmother. She taught me how to be a good woman, always trying to help others and be a positive light in the world. She volunteered, supported numerous charities, and always rescued one cat or another. Ultimately, she ended her journey of life on her terms — sparing the family she loved a prolonged death — with quiet, peaceful, and sweet memories of her final hours.

I hope you read her story to follow. Before doing so, I want to point out that one of the biggest heartbreaks she faced yet neglected to articulate accurately was concerning her inheritance. She was so proud of her father because he became a successful businessman without ever attending one day of high school. He worked hard, intending to care for his family in life and death. It pained her to live the last decade of her life knowing that everything he worked for wound up in the hands of the Polish caretaker, Selena, who was hired to care for my grandmother. We believed her to be a wonderful person caring for grandma so well, but unbeknownst to us, she had done everything legally to change the family's will. We also had to question whether grandma's final passing was organic or assisted by someone who would benefit from her death.

My mom grieved for that injustice and spent thousands of dollars investigating the situation and trying to right that wrong, only giving up when the bills got too high. Since then, the struggles remained for her and Larry, both emotionally and financially, yet neither of them ever gave up.

Your Stories

To include a story or memory you had with Sue in the next edition of this Legacy Journal; please go to **bit.ly/susanjg**

Her family thanks you in advance for your time with this.

One Simple Phrase

National Alliance on Mental Illness

1 in 5 Americans struggle with mental illness.

If you or a loved one struggles with a mental health condition, visit NAMI, the National Alliance on Mental Illness: www.Nami.org

Call or text the NAMI Helpline at 800-950-6264, or chat with us, Monday – Friday, 10 a.m.-10 p.m. (EST)

In a crisis? Call or text 988

One Simple Phrase

Stories Before the Story

Stories about Sue from those who loved her most.

One Simple Phrase

Lawrence Giannini

(Husband)

What can I say about Susan Giannini? Mother, grandmother, stepmom, great-grandmother, my wife, my friend, my lover, and my co-conspirator.

Who knew two people from different backgrounds would find each other and get married? Many people out there said, "you've got to be kidding," but we made it work for thirty-nine years. They were not all great years, but we got through them TOGETHER. We fought, loved, and had fun. We had a great family, good friends, and great times.

Sue was the love of my life and the one person I wanted to spend the rest of my life with. Sue passed away way too soon. I only wish we had more time together.

I miss my best friend, my wife, and I hope, hope, hope, and pray that we will be together again.

One Simple Phrase

Gerald Ruffino

(Grandson)

All I need to say is, "Pancakes at McDonalds every morning before school" From here forward, my go-to spot if we need to talk will be at that McDonalds booth. With you gone, you now KNOW I have the ability to see into the other side, and you KNOW that now! We will meet at the McDonalds booth whenever we need to talk!

One Simple Phrase

Jesica Ruffino

(Granddaughter)

My grandma was one of the sweetest ladies around. She was always thinking about other people and LOVED animals. I remember going to her house as a kid, and she always went out of her way to ensure my brother and I were as happy as possible!

Around Christmas, we would go to my grandma's house to make homemade potato donuts. My Great-Great Grandma Crowley (Sue's Grandma) passed the recipe down. Her house would fill with the smell of donut grease, and the kitchen would have a million sprinkles on the floor, but we all loved this tradition. It brought us close around the  holidays, and we all ate as many donuts as possible until we eventually looked like a donut. This was a tradition we did every year as a family.

One Simple Phrase

Although it will never be the same without her, we will continue to do this as a family, with her looking over us. ♥

You might not be around anymore, but I know you are looking over each and every one of us. I love you sooooo much, and one day we will meet again. I love you to the moon and back.

Jan Blackburn Sawitoski

(Childhood Friend)

Sue and I spent most of our childhood together on Washington Street in Wheaton, Illinois. She was a year ahead of me in school, but that didn't stop us from doing everything together. Bike riding, trick or treating, going to the movies, going out to go dancing (rock and roll), and going to eat French fries and a coke at the Woolworths in Wheaton. We spent time having overnights at each other's homes, going to Michigan to my aunt's house on the train, or going to her Grandparent's house in Iowa.

I remember the year that the Bicentennial in Wheaton was going on and the show that the city put on each night for a week. Sue and I were in it, and we wore Indian costumes. We rode the Wheaton bus to the high school football field area, stayed till late, and then took a bus home. I would not let my kids do that now, but Wheaton, at that time, was a very safe place to be. She even taught me how to whistle (like guys do) on the bus one day.

I sure miss the fun we had and the close friendship we shared. Then we grew up and had families, and distance geographically separated us for far too long!! Miss you Susie

One Simple Phrase

Deana Dolan

(Family Friend)

I have many fond memories of Sue that go way, way back. I dated her son back in the late 80s, which is how my path became intertwined with her family. When first introduced to her, I was welcomed warmly and saw that her wit and sarcastic humor would be her signature. I had family dinners, went on outings, and spent the holidays with all of them for some years. This was how I met Christie, one of my best friends to this day.

I remember Sue's love of Vegas, the color purple/teal, and her overall zest for life and having a good time. I remember going to their house, and their friends Rich and Cindy had parked a camper on their driveway for an upcoming trip… most likely to Iowa or a lake. Upon arriving, the door opens, and out pops Sue… common in Nene, and have a cocktail with us. That's just the kind of person she was. It didn't matter where she was… she always wanted to have fun. One of her favorite things was listening to Johnny B on the radio. Back in the day, he was the hot guy on the radio and took a stab at daytime television. We went downtown to one of the live shows as audience members, and it was so fun… I still vividly remember

One Simple Phrase

it! I wasn't much of a fan before I went on that show, but I was after, thanks to her.

As a staple to her house, anytime I came over, she fed me, and I would sit and talk to her while she floated around in the pool in the backyard and had the funniest conversations. Anytime I got a new kitten, I would bring it to their house so she could meet it... as an avid animal lover, she always enjoyed that. She also always found the best little gifts and stocking stuffers at Christmas, making sure they fit the person who got them.

After her son and I had parted ways, she called me one day and told me that she was upset about what had happened but understood sometimes things don't work out. She wished me the best and said we would always be friends no matter what. I often remember that and how welcoming she and Larry were to me. I feel so grateful that I had the opportunity to know Sue and be part of her family for a time.

More Tributes

"I will never forget our laughs and tears together. Peace be with you."

—Cindy

"Sue was always friendly and a happy person willing to help others. She Will be missed."

—Antoinette

One Simple Phrase

*"Stay strong,
stay positive,
and never give up."*

—Roy T. Bennett

One Simple Phrase

One Simple Phrase

One Woman's Journey to Overcome
Mediocrity and Never Give Up!

By Sue Giannini

One Simple Phrase

One Simple Phrase

It's funny how one simple phrase from childhood can carry you throughout your life. We tell our children many things; *"Look both ways before crossing the street!"*; *"If you can't say something nice, don't say anything at all!"* and *"Don't cross your eyes, or they'll stay that way!"* Some are silly sayings and others are serious about things we hope they'll always remember. We may forget some of them, but others are as clear today as they were when we first heard them in our childhood.

Never Give Up!

"Never Give Up!" was just one of the phrases my father repeated to me as a child. *"Never Give Up, do what you have to do, and if you stumble, Never Give Up."*

I grew up during a time when mental illness and depression weren't very well understood. I was the middle child between two brothers. My childhood was happy enough. However, I could never understand why my mother cried so much. She never talked about it. While I loved my mother and yearned to have a close relationship with her, it was difficult for me to get close to something I couldn't understand. I now realize that my mother suffered from depression.

One Simple Phrase

On the other hand, I was very close to my father. The way he raised me was a blessing in my life. He taught me a lot. One lesson that always stayed with me was to *"Never Give Up!"*

As a child in school, I would continuously whine about schoolwork. My dad would firmly but lovingly say just to go and do it. Thanks to his advice, I received good grades. The one exception was the first semester when I took Algebra and got a F. I wanted to drop the course, but he said "No, don't give up." Sure enough, I hung in there; and in the second semester, everything clicked. I even ended up loving the subject.

I had a good adult life. I got married and had two children, a girl and a boy. Of course, there were some difficult times, like every parent experiences. I got divorced, but unlike many couples, ours was amicable. Since we had children, we both agreed that focusing on the best outcome for them was essential. Nine years later, I married a man who has been a rock throughout all of our years together.

In 1995, several events in rapid succession nearly knocked me off my feet.

First, my father took his life. If that wasn't a crushing blow, my younger brother, Chris, also took his life nine days later. At the same time, my mother was in the hospital having a series of strokes.

I suddenly found myself in a situation where I felt I had no one to lean on. In addition to handling the shock of these sudden losses and grieving for my father and brother, I was faced with the responsibility of settling two estates while tending to my mother, whose health was failing rapidly. This was all in addition to my job, which involved working for an oral surgeon as a dental and anesthetic assistant, with the responsibility of administering IV solutions. Fortunately, I had an understanding boss. Yet I consistently felt overwhelmed and ready to break.

Settling an estate is time-consuming and complicated for anyone. In the mid-1990s, it still involved paper copies and snail mail. Many of the documents weren't always easy to find. The job involved wading through hand-written papers to find bank accounts, insurance policies, and other paperwork. This was a slow and often frustrating process. Not only are you grieving the loss of your loved ones, but examining their personal items, will, insurance, bank accounts, and other things that can often reveal shocking surprises.

One of these surprises came for me when I discovered that I had a brother who had died at birth. He was my parent's first child and only lived three hours after birth. I never knew about him and had no idea what had happened to him or where he might have been buried. Upon further investigation, I found out that his name was Michael, and he had been cremated. An even bigger surprise was that his ashes were still at the mortuary! It was an extremely emotional situation for me. Who doesn't bury their child? How could my mom not have wanted to lay his ashes to rest? Was she ashamed of him? Was he not my father's child? Or was she just too grief-stricken to face the task? These were questions and other sorrows that I had to wrestle with, in addition to everything else.

Settling an estate also opens your eyes to what your siblings are like, especially when money is involved. Chris and I were close, and it hurt terribly to lose him. However, it was the actions of my older brother that dealt another surprising blow. He kept distant and unhelpful despite my many pleas. I desperately needed help sorting out not only two estates but the issues involving my mother's care. He didn't want to be bothered, yet he quickly responded when he felt that things weren't handled correctly. He would criticize my actions and leave me feeling like I was a failure and even more alone in the situation.

Meanwhile, my mother continued having strokes. She now needed more care than I could manage while working and handling the estate details. I decided to hire a live-in caretaker so that she could stay comfortable in her home. She eventually passed in 1998, leaving me reeling from the added responsibility of sorting out another estate and yet another surprise.

My mother had changed her will, leaving everything to her caretaker. The whole time we believed that this woman really cared about my mom and was invested in her well-being, only to find out that she had ulterior motives. At the time, I was unaware that I could have had the situation investigated by senior services. Fortunately, there are laws in place now to protect families from these types of predators.

I still have doubts if my mom's death was truly natural or helped by this terrible person. This caused an even more significant split with my older brother, who thought I should have done more.

Would this be the straw that broke the camel's back? There were so many times when I thought I couldn't continue. I envisioned myself just walking away to let the pieces fall where they may. But I didn't. I kept going.

When I look back on that time, I think, how did I get through it all? It goes back to my father telling me, *"Never Give Up!"*, so I kept going.

I had supportive friends, and my husband, Larry, was a solid rock for me. However, I had difficulty sleeping and began having anxiety attacks. I quickly sank into depression. I knew something was wrong with me. While Larry didn't understand depression, he would sit with me and just listen, holding my hand while I cried. I don't know what I would have done without him.

I knew I needed to learn to calm down and finish the work that I had to do. Depression and mental illness still held a stigma for many people in the 1990s, but fortunately, I didn't feel that way. I wasn't too proud to ask for help. I can't say I'm overly religious, but I do think that I got help along the way from some external force. I knew I needed help and was led to a local crisis center in Lombard.

Still Not Giving Up!

My story doesn't stop there. Recovering from depression is a process, not an overnight miracle. Over the coming years, I would work with various doctors, each one helping me along this journey. I was fortunate to find good doctors that I felt comfortable with. Some of them I still see to this day.

Every day I took another step forward. On some of those days, I could only concentrate on just getting through that day. I was hard on myself, especially when I felt I didn't get things accomplished like I wanted to. I would tell myself that it was OK and there's always tomorrow.

One Simple Phrase

I learned that there are different steps in the process, some of which are not always permanent. For instance, I started a journal, which is an excellent tool for many people. Some people keep journals for years. It helped when I first started, and I found it to be a great way to sort things out. Some of the revelations I had made me realize I should have done things differently. I ended up feeling disgusted with myself and never went back to journaling.

Thankfully, I kept working with my doctors. The biggest challenge I had was letting go of painful memories. I would rehash them over and over again and second-guess my decisions 24/7. It was ruining my life. A counselor gave me one of the best techniques for quieting the continual soundtrack that ran in my head. He told me to look at a situation and treat it like a book. I could open that book every once in a while, then close it and put it up on the shelf, leaving it alone until I felt it was the right time to open it again. Initially, I opened up those books a lot because I didn't want to let go of my feelings. But, I didn't give up. Eventually, I opened the book less and less until I finally recognized I was tired of looking at this book. It was a simple strategy, but it made a big difference in my life.

When my husband retired, we bought a cabin on a river in Iowa. That run-down little cabin turned out to be a savior for both of us. It took us about six months to get it renovated so we could stay there without having to work on it. We loved every single minute we spent there! Every other Thursday, we would leave Chicago and stay through Monday. This little routine gave us both something to look forward to. We had a ball whenever we went there! We loved the area and made so many friends. The cabin held many happy memories that I don't want to forget. Over time, it became too expensive to keep the cabin. However, we still visit our friends there as often as we can.

Those who hear my story find it hard to believe that so many family sorrows, secrets, and surprises didn't completely break me. Looking back now, I realize that I did everything I possibly could. I just kept going. There was no need for me to have been as hard on myself as I was. It was a difficult situation, and I did the best I could. I believe life is a series of tests, and you have to navigate through them one way or another.

Today, I have an optimistic outlook. I've come a long way. It took me a long time, but I'm here. I learned a lot from those horrible, ugly years, and I am proud of myself for that. I am so blessed to have a strong, loving husband, two beautiful and understanding children, three grandchildren, and a delightful little great-granddaughter. I attribute my staying power to family, friends, and excellent doctors.

Never Give Up! The Next Generation

That simple bit of advice given by my father many years ago, not only taught me as a child, but was also passed on to my daughter. I was there for her when she faced difficult times. During a divorce, I was able to be there for her and encourage her to *"Never give up!"* I was able to say and believe that things would get better. They always do. Nothing stays the same.

Today, it is easier to find help when you are struggling with depression or just feeling overwhelmed in general by life's challenging moments. You don't have to do it all by yourself. There are some people still out there that don't believe in counseling or therapy, but I think that way of thinking is to

One Simple Phrase

their detriment. They'll just go on suffering from their thoughts and memories. I encourage anyone reading this not to be too proud or afraid to seek help. Reach out, find a good doctor, and rely on the people you feel comfortable sharing your story with. They can offer you a way through your pain and provide you with coping strategies and ideas. I can't recommend it highly enough.

And, just for good measure, I'll add, *"Never – EVER Give Up!"*

About Sue Giannini

Sue Giannini was born and raised in the Chicago area. She began working for her orthodontist right out of high school. As she became a mother to Christie and Jerry, she was fortunate to remain a stay-at-home mother until they began elementary school. At that point, she returned to her position at the orthodontist's office, where she especially enjoyed working with the children, who made up the majority of the patient load. A few years later, the orthodontist retired, and Sue then joined an oral surgeon. Always fascinated by surgery, Sue obtained a certification in anesthesiology from the University of Chicago. She continued working until her health issues became too challenging. She shares her story of how depression and family secrets and surprises impacted her life.

www.MyLegacyJournal.com/Sue

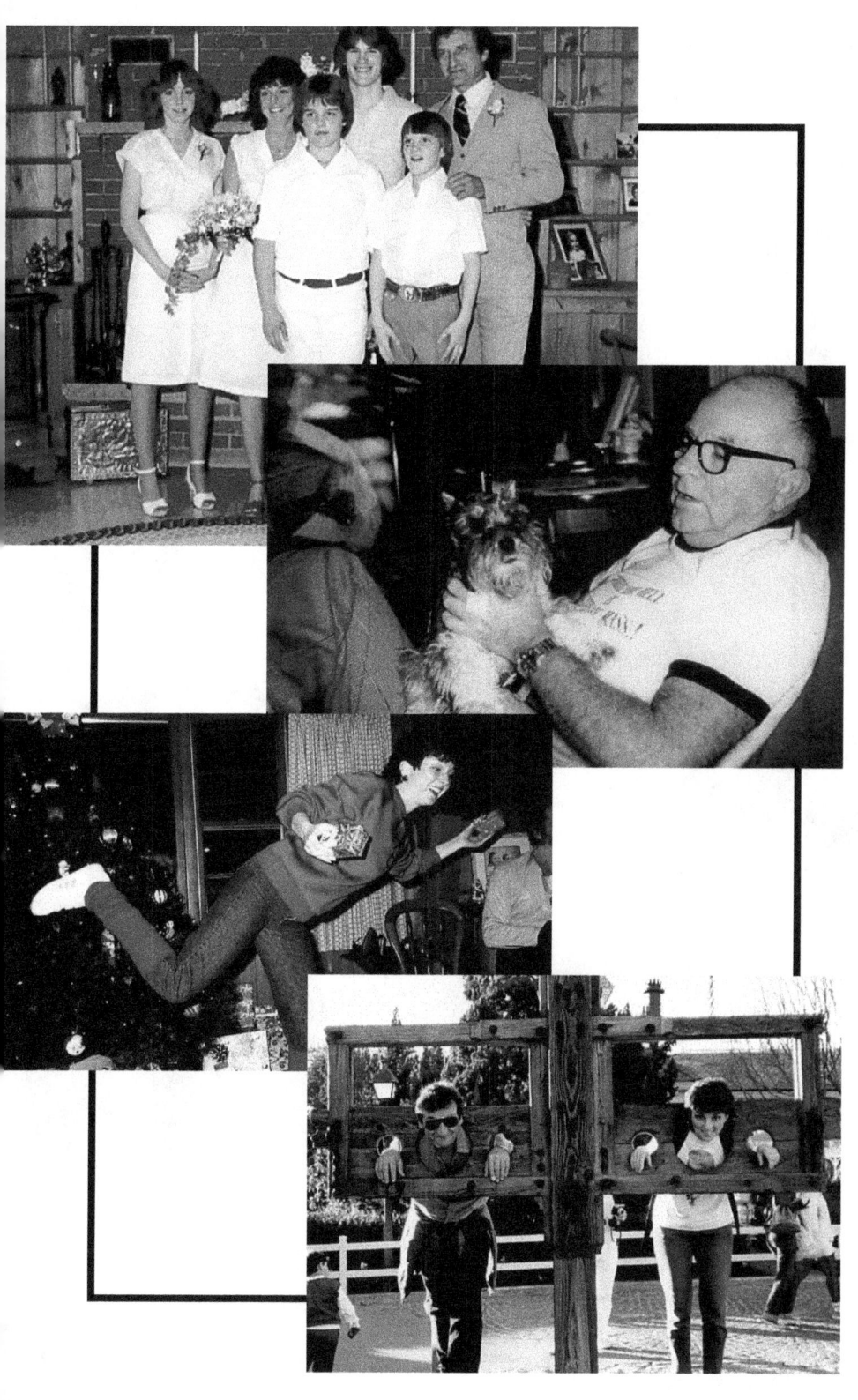

Your Stories About Sue

To include a story or memory you had with Sue in this Legacy Journal, please go to: **bit.ly/susanjg**

Visit:

www.MyLegacyJournal.com/Sue

National Alliance on Mental Illness

1 in 5 Americans struggle with mental illness.

If you or a loved one struggles with a mental health condition, visit NAMI, the National Alliance on Mental Illness: www.Nami.org

Call or text the NAMI Helpline at 800-950-6264, or chat with us, Monday – Friday, 10 a.m.-10 p.m. (EST)

In a crisis? Call or text 988

www.ingramcontent.com/pod-product-compliance
Lightning Source LLC
Chambersburg PA
CBHW072037060426
42449CB00010BA/2315